Ellie's Code

By

ELIANA VILLARROEL

Illustrated by

Mauricio Sanchez-Patzy

Ellie's Code

Text and illustrations copyright © 2008 by Eliana Villarroel

All rights reserved. No part of this book may be reproduced or utilized in any form or by any means, electronic or mechanical, including photocopying, recording, or by any information storage or retrieval system without written permission from the author.

ISBN 978-0-9911507-0-0

Summary and Directions:

The research-based method used in Ellie's Code is designed to teach children and older non-readers, including those with reading and spelling difficulties, learning disabilities, and English language learners, to decode, build fluency, and develop spelling accuracy.

Color-coded words aid the brain to recognize mini-words within words and spelling patterns to process faster. This develops automaticity leading to greater fluency. The word lists are divided into sixteen mini-lists comprised of 128 high-frequency words which correspond to the pages of Ellie's Code, a vocabulary-controlled story about two mischievous ants, a cat, and a rat.

Underlined words on the text need repetition and practice. Words marked with two (**) on the lists are not considered high frequency words.

The student should master reading fluency and spelling of word lists prior to reading the corresponding page text. The student does not need to memorize the code. All dictation and tests are done with a black pencil. The code is used to simplify decoding skills and guide the student to achieve mastery of reading fluency and improve spelling.

Word count is provided for each page. The student should be able to read each page with a reading fluency of at least 70-80 words per minute, prior to continuing to the next page.

Dictation of each word list along with the text page is recommended. One square centimeter graph paper notebook should be used. If the student misses any of the words, first ask him or her to look at the word he/she wrote and find the mistake. Next, ask him/her to close his/her eyes and attempt to self-correct. Then, ask the student to write the word seven times in a column using the corresponding colors and switching color pencils for every word, as necessary. Last, re-test until mastery of each word list is achieved.

When the book is completed, give the reading and spelling test of the complete 132 word list. See Instructional Guide for testing materials, record keeping sheets, more suggestions, and strategies.

Using this color-coded method allows the reader to discover a unique, simple method to decode and spell the English language with ease and enjoyment. There are four additional color-coded stories which are recommended to improve reading fluency: *The Old Wolf and the Three Little Pigs- Level 1 (First Grade), The Old Wolf and the Red Hen - Level 2 (Second/Third Grade), The Old Wolf and Jack and the Beanstalk – Level 3 (Third/Fourth/Fifth Grade),* and *Old Wolf's Search for Pinocchio – Level 4 (Sixth Grade and above).*

For eight years, this method was thoroughly tested and successfully used with hundreds of special education students, English language learners, and students who were identified at risk because of their inability to read and write at grade level.

SUMMARY GUIDE FOR COLOR-CODE USAGE:

COLOR CODE:	USE:	SAMPLES:
BLUE LETTER (S)	■ Identify whole words or mini-words within word(s) and/or spelling patterns which can be easily decoded in isolation.	as, fast, has, all, call, can, the, them, for, only, just, think, story, together, watch, you, before,
GREEN LETTER (S)	■ Complete all the sounds required to decode the word when added to the blue letters and/or the red and green letters. ■ May serve to identify the change of nouns from singular to plural. ■ Regular verb-tense endings: (present progressive, past tense) ■ Adverb endings as needed.	they, was, about, maybe, words, ants legs, pigs, bricks doing, falling, saying, looked, called luckily, proudly
RED LETTER (S)	■ Identify silent letter(s). Important to remember for spelling. ■ May alert the reader to change the previous vowel(s) sound from a short vowel to a long vowel, or vice versa. ■ Guides the reader to focus on decoding the blue short/long vowel, while ignoring the red vowel for vowel digraphs (two successive letters whose phonetic value is a single sound). ■ Help to distinguish the correct meaning of a homophone (Two or more words pronounced alike, but are different in meaning, derivation or spelling.)	one, why, know, watch, school, answered time, made, like, give, have your, yours, could, please, people, thought, because to, too, two - right, write their, there - hear, here

♥

I dedicate my work to the loving memory of my parents,

Carlos Villarroel Soriano and Nelly Blatch-Villarroel.

I also dedicate this book to all my Special Education students

who embraced the challenge to believe in themselves,

conquered their fears, and realized their dreams

to become fluent readers and good spellers.

They inspired me to seek a different way to teach.

I learned from their mistakes.

♥

Word List 1

a

an

and

can

*than

many

want

at

that

what

**water

A cat has a red hat.

That cat is fat.

Can all cats be fat?

The cat called the rat.

The cat is bigger than the rat.

The rat is bigger than the ants.

Word List 2

as

was

has

a**sk**

ple**a**s**e**

had

all

call

*****c**all**e**d

small

That ant was almost as tall as the other ant.

The ants were looking at the rat.

What are the rat and the cat doing?

The rat can see an ant in the water.

She had to call the cat.

Word List 3

she

he

her

he**lp**

get

we

wer**e**

be

be**en**

see

green

keep

The ants can see the cat.

He has his big, red hat.

The ants can call the rat and the cat.

They called them to ask how they had been.

The ants had their fans.

These fans are made of plants.

Word List 4

the

then

them

they

these

*other

there

their

those

They sat on their fans.

Their fans are green.

The rat wanted to see the cat.

She went there to see the fat cat.

Then, she was happy to see those ants.

She gave them some food and asked them,

"What do you want to be if you could be someone else?"

Word List 5

I

is

his

this

wish

him

big

if

of

off

"Today we are happy just to be ants!" answered the ants.

Then, the rat called the cat saying, "This call is from the rat. Tell the cat that I just found his two friends, the ants. I am calling to ask him if he knew that they had run off to play by the water."

Just then, the rat went to look for the cat. By now she was hungry and thought, "I can see two ants on his plants! How I wish these ants were made of candy!"

Word List 6

it

its

again

find

in

into

today

to

too

two

Later, one of the ants fell in the water! It was sad to see her with her eyes shut and falling off her fan. Her fan was sinking into the water.

The other ant went in the water with its fan, too. Now, two ants were in the water! The rat went in the water, too. The ants asked her for help, "Can you please help us find our two fans?"

"Forget the fans! Get on top of my back!" said the rat.

Word List 7

or

for

*more

**words

do

does

did

said

Back on land, one ant said, "I can hear some words far away."

"I can hear them, too!" said the other ant.

"Those are not words! Those are more ants with fans making all that noise! I can see them coming from up here!" the rat said. Then the rat asked, "Do you want to have another fan or did the other ant go up the tree to get a fan, too?"

"She had one or two fans, but they fell into the water and again she went in to get them!" the ant told the rat.

Word List 8

so

soon

some

from

up

but

The rat swam over to look and she saw the small ant in the water. "I told her to be careful, so now what can I do for her? Does she want this fan or that one over there, so she can get on top of it?" asked the rat.

"I have more fans from my sisters," said the ant. The rat gave the two fans to the small ant. "I only want one long fan, not two fans!" said the ant.

Word List 9

on

only

long

one

no

not

look

good

go

Later that day, the cat came by looking for his friends. The rat looked at him and said, "She was here and then she went over there. After that I did not see her anymore. She had the long fan in one hand and the water was going fast! When I looked for her after that, there were other ants over here and over there."

Word List 10

over

after

w**h**er**e**

w**h**en

The other ants came by and said, "We were looking for them for a long time, but no one knew where they were!"

Just then, the cat was about to step on the small ant. The rat had to shout to the cat, "Watch out! Do not step on her!"

The cat took one look at them and after that he said, "Oh, no!" Then he jumped and took off. Where the cat went, no one will ever know!

Word List 11

pretty

very

try

by

my

*way

away

may

say

At last, the small ants were out of the water and safe. The big ants came by to say "Hi!" The little ant did not know where she was when she saw that there were so many ants by her side.

Pretty soon she got up and ran over to ask them, "May I be your friend? I like to meet big ants. I was on my way to school, but I still have some time to make friends. All of you look just like me!"

Word List 12

made

make

have

gave

are

like

**time

little

*people

"People are coming!" shouted one of the big ants. They all called each other to say, "We must all run away!" This made the ants very scared and they did not know which way to go.

Each of the ants dropped its fan and began to run. They ran very fast, but there was no time for all the ants to get away. "We are trying to run as fast as we can!" the little ant said.

Word List 13

use

us

jump

just

must

*most

first

The first big ant said, "We must use our six legs to run. We must get away as fast as we can. Most of us could hide under the plants."

The other big ant said, "You must get your fans and put them on top of your backs! That way, you will all look like a big plant."

Then all the ants shouted, "We think that would be a good idea, we should do it now!"

Word List 14

would

could

you

*your

yours

out

about

The people came by and the ants hid under their fans.

The small ant did not have time to get away and was still hiding under her fan. A man was about to step on her, when all of a sudden, the cat came back. The man turned around to see the cat dancing on two legs on top of his red hat!

"Who is that cat dancing on top of his red hat?" the people asked. Who would have thought that the cat could have such a good plan to make the people turn around and go back?

Word List 15

with

will

who

which

*each

read

In the end, the ant was saved! "How can I thank you, cat, for saving my life?" asked the little ant who was still hiding under her fan.

Then the cat knelt down to shake her hand and replied, "You are welcome! Just be careful the next time you play down by the water! And don't forget to thank the rat! Now you better go. You must get to school on time because today is your spelling test!"

Luckily everyone got to school safe. Then, the rat

Word List 16

know

now

how

own

down

said proudly, "Now with all of this, which I am about to tell each one of you, I know that by now you must know how to read and spell all of your words! You learned it by using Ellie's Code! You should be proud because now you know which letters to use to spell so many words! By now you know how to do it on your own! This story and test is yours to keep and read to someone else."

Then the rat waved good-bye to us saying, "Maybe, just maybe, I will see you someday around the playground."

Printed in Great Britain
by Amazon.co.uk, Ltd.,
Marston Gate.